Life Before You

Eva Hudson

methuen | drama

LONDON • NEW YORK • OXFORD • NEW DELHI • SYDNEY

METHUEN DRAMA

Bloomsbury Publishing Plc, 50 Bedford Square, London, WC1B 3DP, UK
Bloomsbury Publishing Inc, 1359 Broadway, New York, NY 10018, USA
Bloomsbury Publishing Ireland, 29 Earlsfort Terrace, Dublin 2,
D02 AY28, Ireland

BLOOMSBURY, METHUEN DRAMA and the Methuen
Drama logo are trademarks of Bloomsbury Publishing Plc.

First published in Great Britain 2026

Cover design and image by Malcolm Reid

A catalogue record for this book is available from the British Library.

A catalog record for this book is available from the Library of Congress.

ISBN: PB: 978-1-3506-3427-5
ePDF: 978-1-3506-3428-2
eBook: 978-1-3506-3429-9

Series: Modern Plays

Typeset by Mark Heslington Ltd, Scarborough, North Yorkshire

For product safety related questions contact
productsafety@bloomsbury.com.

To find out more about our authors and books visit
www.bloomsbury.com and sign up for our newsletters.

Life Before You

Life Before You was developed in Bristol by writer Eva
Hudson with director Roisin McCay-Hines, originally seed-
funded by a bursary from Shakespeare at the Tobacco
Factory. Inspired by their shared experiences of navigating
medical misogyny, understandings of class and female
identity, they also share the specific context of being
daughters of Northern Irish mothers who moved to England
and raised their children here. Following a sold-out work-in-
progress run at the Alma Theatre in 2023, the production
received strong programming interest, leading to this UK
tour with a newly developed script and expanded creative
team.

The world premiere of *Life Before You* was presented by
REMH Productions at Theatre Royal Bath on 12 February
2026, followed by a national tour. The production visited
Exeter Northcott and Barnfield Theatres, Sterts Arts Centre,
The Poly, The Acorn Theatre, Theatre Royal Plymouth,
Mercury Theatre Colchester, The Corn Hall, Tobacco
Factory Theatres and The Old Joint Stock.

For my mother, and her mother,
and our mothers' mothers' mothers

With thanks to:

Mum, Dad and Niall

Roisin McCay-Hines and the *Life Before You* team

Larry and Claire Burke

The Kelly Girls

David Lane and the Bristol Old Vic Writers' Class of 2023

Lydia McKinley

Hélène and Manon Théodoly

Neil Norman

Maisie, Milly, Jen, Paola and Hannah

And Elizabeth Wendon-Kerr, for all of the work she does advocating for women's healthcare

Roisin – Director and Producer's Note

Eva and I met during our respective training at Bristol Old Vic Theatre School and quickly became collaborators and, more importantly, friends. From the moment I first read her work, I was struck by her precision and emotional acuity. Her writing is tenacious, intelligent and profound – holding space for tenderness and tension, for what is spoken and what is left unsaid. Eva's work challenges its collaborators to be brave and to meet the provocations of the text with the same courage she brings to writing them. At the same time, it trusts its audience implicitly, inviting us to sit with complexity, contradiction, and the quiet fractures that shape relationships.

Working with Eva has been a journey of shared discovery. Our collaboration, rooted in our intertwined experiences of female identity, class and Northern Irish heritage, has shaped the development process and informed every creative choice. Together, we have explored how Gráinne and Eimear's story – of love, sacrifice and the pressures women inherit – can resonate authentically on stage, capturing both intimacy and universality.

Our rehearsal room has been guided by listening, trust and collaboration, allowing the actors to inhabit the text fully while honouring its structure and rhythm. The production has grown from its seed-funded development in Bristol to, more than two years later, a UK tour with a new script and renewed energy behind it.

A playtext is a beautiful contradiction, capturing something intended to be lived in performance within the static form of print, yet to me this publication serves as an important milestone in the play's ongoing journey, and I look forward to all it is yet to become. I hope it challenges, unsettles and moves you, as it has all of us who have been part of its creation.

Creative Team and Cast

Writer: Eva Hudson

Director and Producer: Roisin McCay-Hines

Designers: Jasmine Thompson and Abigail Manard

Producer Mentor: Emma Gibson

Dramaturgy Mentor: Sarah Dickenson

Technical Stage Manager: Louis Gulliver King

Assistant Director: Izzy Ponsford

Gráinne: Hayley-Marie Axe

Eimear (multirole): Georgia Alexandra

Writer – Eva Hudson

Eva (b. 2001) is an English-Irish writer and director, who studied English Language and Literature at University College London, before training as a playwright at Bristol Old Vic Theatre School.

Her recent work as playwright includes *855-FOR-TRUTH,* which played at The Bridge Theatre, Brussels in May/June 2025, after an initial run at The Hope Theatre, London in January 2025. Her writing has previously been staged at Bristol Old Vic, The Pleasance, London and at the Edinburgh Festival Fringe, and she has additionally directed projects at The Hope Theatre, Arcola Theatre and at the Edinburgh Festival Fringe.

A writer/director for screen, Eva's award-winning short film, *I Knew Her Before She Was A Virgin*, played at eleven film festivals in 2024 and 2025. She is currently developing a feminist comedy-horror for TV and is working on several original series concepts.

As co-founder and artistic director of theatre and film production company Gentlewomen Production House, Eva has also produced theatre and short films across the UK and Europe, and is particularly interested in creating work which centres young people's perspectives in a rapidly changing world, and amplifying voices of young women and marginalised gender identities.

She is longlisted for the Theatre503 International Playwriting Award and is selected for the Exeter Northcott Writer Programme.

Director and Producer – Roisin McCay-Hines

Roisin is a Cornish-Irish director and producer who studied at the University of Exeter before training as a director at Bristol Old Vic Theatre School. She is a recipient of the

Michael Grandage Company Futures Award, Shakespeare at Tobacco Factory Bursary Award and was shortlisted for BBC New Creatives.

Directing credits include *Kevrin: Out of Season* (South West tour, featured in *The Guardian*'s top shows); *Cold, Dark Matters* (Theatre503, The Hope Theatre and Edinburgh Festival Fringe); *Mo Chara, Dia Duit* (Theatre Royal Plymouth); *The Fall of the House of Usher* (Red Rope Theatre); *A Summer of Birds* (Exeter Northcott Theatre); *The Hound of the Baskervilles* (Red Rope Theatre); *Bar Tape* (South West tour); *No One Will Tell Me How to Start a Revolution* (Wardrobe Theatre) and *Pascoe's Pilchard Palace* (Kneehigh).

Assistant director credits include *The Ugly Duckling* (Kneehigh/Wise Children); *Grief Play* (Kneehigh, workshop); *Further Than the Furthest Thing* (Minack Theatre) and *Marthusow ha Mysteris* (Hall for Cornwall / O-region).

As a producer, she leads REMH Productions, developing and touring new work across the UK. Former producing and artist development roles have included the Royal Shakespeare Company, Bristol Old Vic Theatre School and Wiltshire Creative. For Wiltshire Creative, she continues to champion opportunities for freelancers and young people as a trustee.

Designer – Jasmine Thompson

Jasmine is a set and costume designer for live performance. She is heavily influenced by fine art references, distinct use of colour and the natural world. Her primary experience is in outdoor theatre productions, including Pendley Open-Air Shakespeare Festival. Jasmine holds a BA in Costume Production from Arts University Plymouth and an MA in Performance Design from Bristol Old Vic Theatre School.

Designer – Abigail Manard

Abigail is a UK based theatre and film designer. They studied at Baldwin Wallace University where they received two BAs in Design and Technical Theatre and Acting and Directing before coming over to the UK and graduating from Bristol Old Vic Theatre School in 2023 with a MA in Performance Design. Recent productions include *Gurt Haunted* (Bristol Old Vic – Weston Studio and South West tour); *The Rainbow Crossing Academy* (Slick Films); *Earthquakes in London*, *A Dream*, *Nell Gwynn*, *The Sweet Science of Bruising* (The Royal & Derngate) and *Hang* (London Independent Pictures).

Producer Mentor – Emma Gibson

Emma is a people-centred, values-driven producer with over twenty-five years' experience devising, marketing, developing and delivering cultural experiences, audiences and people.

Her work for WildWorks includes *Souterrain* (Dolocath Mine Cornwall); *The Beautiful Journey* (Devonport and Tynemouth Dockyards) and *The Enchanted Palace* (Kensington Palace). For Miracle Theatre, ten years as Communications Director, productions include *Waiting for Godot* (Live and Digital); *The Third Policeman* and *Dr Livingston I Presume!*

Other roles and projects include Associate Director of the Minack Theatre; work with Kneehigh Theatre on *Blast!* and *Brief Encounter*; Director of the TipofyourTongue Poetry Festival and Creative Mentor for The Writers Block, The Works (Dance Theatre Agency Cornwall) and Creative Skills. Most recently, she has been Head of Culture and Community for St Ives Town Council, instigating a new programme of live theatre and literary events, youth programme and revitalising the Guildhall venue.

Dramaturgical Mentor – Sarah Dickenson

Brought up in North Cornwall, Sarah is a writer and dramaturg with over two decades of experience developing new plays nationally and internationally. As dramaturg she is currently working on projects with Paines Plough, Nottingham Playhouse, Chichester Festival Theatre, Jennifer Jackson and Tilted.

Her previous roles have included Associate Dramaturg for Paines Plough, Associate Dramaturg for LAMDA, Associate Dramaturg for the RSC, Production Dramaturg for Shakespeare's Globe, Senior Reader at Soho Theatre, Literary Manager for Theatre503, New Writing Associate at The Red Room. She has been dramaturg on performance projects and artist development nationally and internationally for organisations and theatre makers including the Royal Shakespeare Company, Shakespeare North, Theatre Royal Bury St Edmund's, The Minack, Nuffield Theatre Southampton, Theatre Centre, National Theatre, Bristol Old Vic, Theatre Bristol, Old Vic New Voices, Liverpool Everyman, Theatre Royal Bath, Plymouth Theatre Royal, Tamasha, Apples and Snakes, Almeida, Hall for Cornwall, The Fence and Churchill Theatre Bromley.

As playwright credits include *The Commotion Time* (Exeter Northcott); *From The Horse's Mouth* (O-Region); *Come to Where I'm From* (Paines Plough); *North Ealing* (Theatre503/Rose Bruford); *PowerPlay* (Hampton Court); *Everything's Fine* (co-writer book, Tilted Co). She is a recipient of 2025 Playwright 73 award from the Peggy Ramsay Foundation with Exeter Northcott and Shakespeare's Globe and was awarded a 2025 Olwen Wymark Theatre Encouragement award for her dramaturgical work with neurodivergent playwrights.

Technical Stage Manager – Louis Gulliver King

Louis Gulliver King is a theatre maker and production manager. He has toured extensively across the UK and internationally as both a performer and technician. Over the last ten years he has been awarded several artist residencies, including a grant from the Artists International Development Fund to train alongside Polish theatre company, Gardzienice. More recently he was involved in lighting the Pyramid Stage at Glastonbury Festival for the 2025 opening ceremony, and was part of the team delivering Jordan Rakei's sell out shows at the Royal Albert Hall. He leads The Rat Affair and runs his own recording studio, The Calf House, in West Cornwall.

Assistant Director – Izzy Ponsford

Izzy Ponsford is a theatre director, assistant director and movement practitioner trained on the MA Contemporary Theatre Directing at Rose Bruford College. Her practice spans devised theatre, new writing and community work, and is informed by ongoing research into textiles and weaving as tools for storytelling, community and change.

Cast

Gráinne – Hayley-Marie Axe

Hayley's Theatre credits include Mrs Higgins in *Pygmalion*, Andy in *Stepping Out* (Frinton Summer Theatre); Linda in *Leave a Message* (The Vaults); Mary in *Baby Blues* (Cheltenham Everyman Theatre); Nurse Ratched in *One Flew Over the Cuckoo's Nest* (Customs House Theatre); Hippolyta in *The Two Noble Kinsmen* (Theatre Royal Bath, Ustinov Studio); Eleanor Dashwood in *Sense and Sensibility* (UK tour); Lesley in *Talking Heads*, Marie D'Amour in *Paris Snow* the musical and Shelley in the comedy *Ladies Day* – for which she was awarded Broadway Baby's best supporting actress award.

TV credits include series regular Big Dan in *Mudtown*, *Say Nothing*, *The Devil's Hour*, *Red Dwarf* TV special and series XII, *Silent Witness*, *EastEnders*, *Tricky TV*, *Vice Squad: NYC* and TV pilot *These Four Sides*.

Film credits include *The Gun Man* (award-winning short); feature films include *Dungeons and Dragons: Honour Amongst Thieves*, *Les Parfaits* (release 2026). Hayley also played the female lead Val Stone in the multi-award-winning Brit comedy feature film *May I Kill U?* written and directed by two-times BAFTA winner Stuart Urban.

Eimear (multirole) – Georgia Alexandra

Georgia trained at Arts University Bournemouth, graduating in 2022.

Her credits include *Call the Midwife* (BBC) for TV, and *A London Lark Rising* (Butterfly Theatre Company), a site-specific production.

Life Before You is her professional stage debut and she is delighted to be a part of this moving and imperative story.

Acknowledgements

Life Before You was produced by REMH Productions supported using public funding by Arts Council England, Shakespeare at the Tobacco Factory Fund, and in-kind support by Shoreditch Town Hall. The production proudly supported The Menopause Charity.

With additional thanks to Lucy Mabbitt, Tom Clay, Helen Birchenough, Doric Bossom, Ben Kernow, Emma Rice Company, Bristol Old Vic Theatre School and Hall for Cornwall for their unwavering support of the production, and the whole team behind it.

Life Before You

Characters

Gráinne, *43, Northern Irish – (female)*

Eimear, *18, English – (female)*

Doctor *(male)*, **Mam** *(female)*, **Mam's Husband**, **Fenella**, **Butcher Shop Man**, *and Tom's* **women** *should each be played by Eimear, unless their lines are reported speech, remembered or recounted by Gráinne and Eimear, as themselves. Although these characterisations must be believable, this is not, flatly, the actor multi-roleing; there must be some sense or ambiguity that this is – in some way – Eimear becoming the characters. Something of Eimear must linger.*

A note on staging

In whatever way Gráinne disappears, it should be felt and real and unreal. Whether a trick of lighting, or of the set, or a choice the director makes entirely separate from these suggestions – it should feel like her surroundings and circumstances are swallowing or vanishing her. It should skate along the line of feverish or imagined and real. It happens in the heat of her hot flushes but there are factors that lead to it. The home she didn't choose. Not being listened to. Not being believed.

The threshold to each room is like the threshold to the female body and the histories there contained. The walls must – in some way – physically move.

Punctuation

A forward slash (/) indicates overlapping or interruption of speech.

A comma on its own line (,) indicates a beat, a breath, a shift in thought.

Words in parentheses () are swallowed, mumbled or sometimes omitted. Or if spoken loudly there is a sense that they are difficult to say.

Speech by different characters on the same line should be spoken at the same time.

Please note: This script went to print before rehearsals and may differ to the text performed.

Act One

Prologue

Reigate, Surrey. Present day.

An upper-middle-class English kitchen: whatever this means to you. The home originally belonged to Tom's family, though **Gráinne** *has made some efforts over the years to make it her own. These efforts feel, in some way, strained or performed. On the island is a bowl overflowing with oranges, an empty vase, and a pile of raw steak. A Scrabble set is somewhere in the room.*

Pride of place is a beautiful painting of Paris, made from shards of objects.

In the kitchen is **Gráinne**, *43. Uncomfortable, she is trying to get cool.*

Eimear, *18, is somewhere outside the walls. Her art materials close by, she is recording herself.*

Gráinne *pushes through the heat and hum of panic, comforted by early memories of* **Eimear**.

Gráinne   For you, it is, I give you name. You wear it now as you did lying on my chest. Now as then, as you leave, the car door shuts; now like then in the pores of your skin. Stretched over little bones I formed now formed of you.

An explosion, it was, as my banks burst, and you came into life.

'What's her name', your father's mother asked me. One thing I am allowed to pick.

Gráinne   'Eimear,   **Eimear**   Eimear Dav/(ies)
After the lady works down
Dunnes Stores'

Eimear   Student number 571/83

Gráinne   'Eimear like the wife of Cuchulainn'

Eimear, well, the name just *arrived* in my head and you took to it; it took to you. Fit you so well.

Eimear   Everyone says they don't remember being a baby but I do.

I remember every part of it. I remember being born.

Gráinne   Forgot all about the pain soon as your soft cheek touched mine.

I stayed an hour and a day, you lying on my chest. Didn't want to go back to Tom's Mam's noo I preferred the smell of Dettol bleach on the ward to the sight of her horrible wallpaper. Wanted it to be just us –

But still, I was driven here . . .

She offers me an apple. Tom's Mam does I demand a ripe packet of cheese and onion crisps. Look her in the eyes those posh narrow English eyes and Crunch Crunch in protest.

Eimear   I think actually, if you think about it, I probably gave birth to myself.

Gráinne   Your hair was so SPIKY. Looked like a little Boxer. Tom's Mam asked *'which do you mean the dog or the fighter'* and to be honest I meant both.

You came out with so much liquid. Water, blood, tears, amazing, really, how we lose that, and we just make more. Amazing. You were, Eimear. Still are.

Rain now

From streetlamps

as the cord is cut from me again

Water under car wheels; bounced down from the wingmirror's edge

My home can't carry you; can't contain you?

Eimear   There's a decision there, isn't there. To like, Turn your head around. I think we all deserve so much more credit for being born.

Gráinne   Whatever she has of Tom, she has Irish eyes. Bright and round and full of water and feeling. She took me in immediately; saw me;

Eimear   I Think She Thinks I don't know her body was hijacked by me.

Gráinne   Back home they're praying so hard their knees are red. At home the sacred heart lamp wonders where you are. At home they keep the death box ready just in case. Home. Here?

Eimear   Is that why she left? Won't talk about Ireland much?

Gráinne   She used to see me.

Eimear   As perfect.

Gráinne   Used to look at me

Eimear   That way

Gráinne   Where did I go w/rong?

Eimear   Where did I go wrong?

Together

Gráinne *is exhausted but completely besotted with her baby* **Eimear***.*

The two are cocooned by the walls of the home, as they move through CHILDHOOD. They are held together somehow by the house.

Eimear   DADDY DADDY Dad Dad DADDY

Gráinne   I dress you; I feed you; I bathe you and your first words are

Eimear   Daddy, DADDY, DaddddddDADDY

Gráinne   He's in Japan. He's in Oslo. He's in Stockholm.
(Thank God I have you).

＊

Eimear *is six and is tracing her mum's face with her hand.*

Eimear   What do you want to be when you grow up.

Gráinne   I'm your Mummy.

Eimear   I WANT TO BE A PAINTER.

＊

Eimear *is seven and crying uncontrollably.*

Gráinne   What is it, what is it, darling?

In between long sobs.

Eimear   I DON'T HAVE A BEST FRIEND.

Beat.

Gráinne   I'll be your best friend.

Oh my wee angel, I'll Be Your Best Friend.

We'll go into town together.

Our life is just beginning, pet.

＊

Eimear *is eight.*

Gráinne   First Christmas just the two of us. First Christmas
Tom was stuck in –?

Eimear   Lapland

Gráinne   no   **Eimear**   Libya?

Gráinne   Latvia for work. Lifted you up to the top of the tree, not even light now. And you, Eimear, were our angel decoration.

*

Eimear *is now nine.*

Eimear   For my homework I have to draw a picture of how you two met

Gráinne (*immediately*)   Here in Reigate –

Eimear   In the house?

Gráinne   At a skiing convention for people who – ski.

Eimear   You're always just in the house.

Gráinne   In a . . . Waitrose – chutney aisle. Boden. A White Company –

Eimear   BORING

Gráinne   Eimear

Eimear   BORING Tell Meeeee

Gráinne   In a Butcher's shop, Eimear

Eimear   Buying steak?

Gráinne   I was poor, living at home, earned my keep scrubbing Butcher's trays. And your Daddy, Heroic Peace Time Soldier as he was, took a fancy.

Eimear   *Fancy* stea/k?

Gráinne   Wanted a go with the Catholic girl. Novelty points. How's that. I was bored and lonely and sad. He was excitement in my life. Sold me the dream after of a better life for you after and I couldn't handle Mammy's shame – Is that what you want to hear, pet. I'd take BORING over –

Eimear *pauses and thinks. She makes an assessment based on the vibe of her drawing.*

Eimear   I'll just put . . . swimming the *channel*.

Gráinne   'It's always sunny, and never cold. It's full of happy people and there are no bombs. There are beaches and coconuts and –'

Could have slapped him.

'You're showing, Gráinne. What choice do you have.

You're huge.'

Eimear *starts drawing the story.*

Eimear   'Blossoming, blooming huge

Surrey. It's like Marbella but better.

Marry me, Gráinne.'

Gráinne   He has no ring.

Eimear   Reigate; you'll bloody love it.

*

Eimear *is eleven.*

Silence, as the two of them are so concentrated, playing Scrabble, cuddled. **Gráinne** *plays with* **Eimear**'s *hair.*

Eimear   When do you think is a good time to start having sex

Gráinne *stares at her.*

Gráinne   What did you just ask me

Eimear   We're learning about it at school.

Gráinne   I know. I read the letter. You're eleven.

Eimear   Arabella said she's going to wait until she's at least fourteen, but Candida Grace said she probably won't.

*

Eimear *is now fourteen. She is wearing a risky makeup look, home from school.*

Gráinne *greets her with a smile that says, 'you look amazing'.*
Eimear *avoids her gaze.*

Gráinne   If they've been mean to you I swear to God I'll headbutt them

Eimear   They haven't. They just said my face is a four out of ten.

Gráinne   They're jealous

Eimear   They're being objective.

Gráinne   Yeah well. Arabella is overweight and Candida's mother has a designer vagina.

Beat.

I shouldn't have said that.

Eimear *wipes her makeup off.* **Gráinne** *tries to stop her and comfort her.* **Eimear** *runs out of her Mum's arms.*

*

Eimear *is seventeen. She comes home from school, unpacking her bag.* **Gráinne** *waits excitedly with a large red dress.*

Gráinne   It's time you have it.

She holds it out for her.

My debs dress. Yours now. Had it made for me from Mam's own dress at your age.

You'll have all these events to wear it to soon.

Eimear   Oh my God Mum, are you sure?

Gráinne   It'll look perfect. It's yours now, pet.

Eimear   Wow, I –

Eimear *slips it on or holds it over her uniform.*

Gráinne   Gorgeous. All the balls you might be going to. Stunning!

Eimear *gives her a huge hug.*

Eimear   Thank you, thank you, I love you –

Gráinne   Can I see it. Your portfolio.

Eimear   – Oh, no, I'm sorry –

Gráinne   I could help with your personal stateme/nt –

Eimear   I don't want you to if that's – It's too personal

*

Eimear *is eighteen and three months. Clutching an acceptance letter or email, she is elated.*

Eimear   I got in

Gráinne   What

Eimear   To Oxford. To Art School. I got in. To the Ruskin.

Fuck

I mean –

Gráinne   Don't swear –

Eimear   MUM WHAT THE FUCK I GOT IN TO OXFORD

Gráinne *all of a sudden starts screaming her lungs out. It is inappropriate.*

Eimear   I GOT IN

*

It is the day **Eimear** *leaves. Bags packed, by the door.*

Gráinne   I don't want you to go.

I know it's selfish.

I don't mean that

You've just.

What will I do with my day. Now there's only work.

Eimear   I'll call you. Every day.

Gráinne   You've got a knot in your hair

She combs it out quickly.

Do you promise

Eimear   Of course. I love you more than anyone or anything.

Eimear *starts to walk to the door.* **Gráinne** *races to her.*

Gráinne   Don't forget your orange!

Beat.

You're sure you don't want to be dropped?

Eimear *nods, smiles, takes it and walks to the door. She's almost out of it.*

Gráinne   I wanted to be a painter. When I grew up.

Eimear *turns.*

Eimear   Sorry?

Gráinne   I said I love you. Very much.

She watches **Eimear** *leave.*

Gráinne *goes towards the painting of Paris.*

Where did she go, that girl? Tidy up your paints there, pet.

Apart

The kitchen walls have shifted, closing **Gráinne** *in, opening the stage to reveal a world outside, that* **Eimear** *can walk around, and* **Gráinne** *doesn't have full, free movement around.*

Gráinne *sits in the kitchen. Calling* **Eimear***. We feel the silence now that she's gone.*

No answer.

A day passes.

Two days pass. We see **Gráinne** *grow more and more feverish. Puts her hand to her head, curious.*

She keeps calling.

No answer.

A whole minute passes, where she is just calling.

Calling again.

And again.

And again.

Gráinne   I've taken up cleaning.

It's not something I did much before Eimear left except for when her posh friends came round from school or her Dad comes back from business trips, and we always had the cleaners.

He's missed a few payments into my account the last few months, so I've been picking up extra online work.

Normally works simple. He sends the money for Eimear; she gets the life she deserves, I get a *wee* bit, and in return . . . I just don't ask any questions. But sure he's been busy with work, and.

I couldn't pay the cleaners on time, so they dropped our house from the round.

I've cleaned the island six times and the ceiling twice. I've bleached and sanded

Scraped and skivvied and gutted

Every crevice and surface

And I fill my time with Scrabble.

I play against myself. Sometimes.

Let's face it. All the time.

I quit book club soon as Eimear left.

Was only in it 'cause I wanted her to think I have half a brain. Interests. Hobbies.

And it's not that I don't. I do.

I just couldn't stand the women in it.

'Fenella, how did you give birth to your darling Candida-Grace?'

With her vagina. How the fuck else.

'Was half water bath. Half jelly bath. Was wonderful. She just glided out. My husband Alfie held my hand the whole time and little Johnny made me the most beautiful hummus and falafel sandwich. Said Mummy, aren't you beautiful, as he fed it to me in little pieces. He was only one!'

I gave birth like a normal person. In a normal hospital. And shat myself whilst doing it.

I have taken up cleaning, since Eimear left me. Cleaning and talking to myself.

*

She sits by the phone and waits.

Gráinne   I called her every day.

At first she was delighted.

She'd cry, and we'd FaceTime and I'd eat toast whilst she made hers and we'd laugh at the girls in her college who couldn't pronounce her name.

'How quaint! Is that foreign?'

It's Irish.

'How cute!'

But she got busy. Workload.

Sorry Mummy. You know I love you?

How's Dad? How's his promotion?

He hasn't answered my calls, Mummy.

*

She's scrubbing the house.

Stops and sniffs bleach. Rocks it, watching the liquid swell, rise, fall.

She's turned the house inside out to clean it.

Her phone rings.

She can't find it.

She's tearing everything apart to look for it.

It rings out.

She bursts into tears and rises hot.

She keeps cleaning. She accidentally pours a bit of bleach onto her hand and arm, missing the sponge as she grows hotter.

She puts her arm out, searching for her phone.

For a second, it's like her arm slightly disappears into the sofa.

But we don't really register it. Just a quick 'that felt weird'. Grips her phone.

She phones and rings and phones.

*

Eimear, *in Oxford.*

Eimear   I don't know if she knows deep down but my portfolio is all pictures of her. It's my thing I guess, portraits of my Mum. I've been so excited to show them. To people who actually know.

They've gone down well. But one girl said they're all anti-feminist because they're made of materials from the home. I agreed even though I shouldn't have.

It started with this picture of Paris – pride of place in our house. She looks to it every day. It's where my mixing of objects started –

I have a big final term project and I have no idea what to paint. Ever since I've left I can't paint her in so much detail?

I miss her. But try not to rely too much on her, dwell; try and embrace what it is to be here.

Eimear *sees some girls walking past from her class.*

Is anyone going to the pub later?

I had. I had plans anyway

We move with her to an art crit.

Yeah, so –

Her mum is calling her. She silences the call.

Yeah, so my portrait this week is of her again. They're um always kind of of my Mum.

Since I've been here I haven't been able to paint with the same, like, specificity? – it's like the distance has . . .

Yeah so in this one she um has steak for a head: any questions?

Oh,

You think it's. Strange? That I only paint her? Oh, I hadn't thought of it like that . . .

Yeah. You're probably righ – Next Week I'll Paint Something Else.

Eimear *goes back into her room and gets her recording device out.*

I've taken up . . . recording myself.

Just checking I sound okay before I present my work. Or um. Me.

Practice my next presentation and asking people to the pub. The work is intense, but I find the confidence to ask harde –

(would you like . . . are you free . . . do you wannnaaaa . . . *fuck's sake.*)

The Art Crit is something we practiced at school, but Ruskin is new heights. The girls here are *different.* They know their Manet from their Monet and down wine like it's water. They're so *in their bodies* and have had four Proper Real Boyfriends each. They say words like *phenomenological* and *steezy* in the same sentence. They have huge friend groups and loads of texts that aren't from their Mums.

I'm shitting myself.

I feel . . . embarassed.

I feel . . . twee.

She declines a call from her mum.

I'm Eimear. *Sick* to meet you – Eimear. Yeah.

(Yeah true steak not very environmental. You're right. Tilda? Sick name. Hey. Hi. *Stoked* to meet you)

(And if anyone wants to say hi or go to the pub or Whatever I am um very Up Very Keen for That)

Gráinne   I know she's better off
there

And I should get a new hobby.

Phone up the school mums

Beg to hear about tennis and tax
evasion

           Eimear   It Is All Fine.

           I am learning so, so much

           the girls here are nice

           but they move with such

           assurance like they've never

           doubted themselves ever.

           I might get a mullet and a knife
           tattoo

           I might dye my hair purple

           Or wear a rugby shirt and get really
           into rowing

I meet Tilda every day before our lectures. We go in together and if she's late I save her seat. She can't say my name so I don't know why but I said it's Emma? Said it's an error on the system because she looked so grossed out trying to say the letters togeth – So now everyone thinks my name is Emma.

Her projects are amazing. Her Thing is all Women and Invisible Labour: in places like Nicaragua their work goes unseen and she's trying to draw attention to that through her art. I wish I saw things like that instead of just looking at what's in front of me.

I'm at the pub some days and some days not; she doesn't always invite everyone –

I'm not unpopular but I'm not not –

Eimear *begins to distract herself by painting. She is painting* **Gráinne***'s lower body, starting with her legs.*

Each time I paint there's something new I can't get right. Paint her shoes, her shins, her calves –

Text Mum the odd life update: 'have a new friend called Tilda. Seeing a boy had one one night stand.'

Just normal things you tell your Mum

Gráinne   I know I should probably call the doctor

My fevers are getting more frequent

But Mammy's voice says *get on with it girl*

I don't know if it's just because she's gone

But I feel this physical sense of

Heat and

Of going

> **Eimear**   I just wish I could grow up.
>
> Grow out of it.
>
> I just can't help but feel I have betrayed her by leaving.

Gráinne's *leg disappears.*

And then comes back into view.

Eimear *sees Tilda walk past her window.*

> **Eimear**   TILDA WAIT I'LL COME TOO!

*

Gráinne *hovers over the phone.*

She traces it with her hand.

She decides not to pick it up.

Then does. Calls Tom. He doesn't pick up.

A silence, as she settles still.

Gráinne   My predicament.

Beat. Perhaps she clears her throat.

I think I am turning fucking transparent.

Tries to play it off like a joke.

Or disappearing. Dunno which.

Can't work out if it's something to be upset about.

I look down and my arm's not there or my –

Can't work it out. So far it's just small bits. And they seem to come back so(?)

I don't know if my memories and my love will disappear with my brain or if the soul is actually in the spine or in my ass (or something).

I know it's bad when she's not here. I think that's when it started.

I know it's coming when I rise all hot.

I know it's bad the longer I have been since Tom has cared to call.

Maybe-it's-my-wrinkles-or-just-not-being-useful-or-good-or-clever-as-a-Mam-or-in-the-words-I-use, or as-a-taxi, or a womb or something but

I'm barely here

She picks up the phone.

*

Eimear *arrives at her uni room drunk.*

Eimear   I wear the rugby shirt a big scarf and baggy jeans. Just enough makeup to look like I didn't try. We talk about Heidegger and airbrush, country houses, Kendall Jenner and North Korea. I think I've cracked her. Tilda.

She's given me six books about environmental art and set me up with her fit friend Henry. I said I'm sick of just painting the same thing so she's invited me to her parents' holiday place in Nicaragua.

I feel like tonight she really saw me.

I think I have a best friend.

,

Yeah no that's cool I had plans anyway Tilda, I'll see you guys tomorrow. Henry? Yeah no. He hasn't replied but I'm sure he will. I'd have gone home with him if he asked I wasn't weird about that (I'm not frigid)

,

Love you.

,

My passport? Yeah. Um. I'll uh . . . for the flights yeah. I'll . . . send it.

She gets her art materials out.

I just can't make anything I like. The more time I spend away from Her the weirder they get.

Bits of her body I keep around the studio. Embroidered bones; sketches of muscles; painted limbs blown apart I hang around the space, jutting out and stretched across the wall. Why do I keep drawing her so . . . dismembered? Bombed out?

I said I'd make something different; I should make something –

She starts painting/making. We see little objects she has from home. She breaks them apart and tries to form a landscape.

Oxford. Fold orange peel into college spires; scrabble shards into riverbeds; doubling; layering; until there's a likeness;

but it's wrong; it's unbalanced;

my hands are moving to fix what failed before. A figure, they fold kitchen metal to create a woman. Her. Her shape is forming. In the bottom corner. No no try to make it different but no matter what it looks like her. She is in everything I draw . . . *Fuck's sake.*

But it's better. It looks better.

I can't separate. I can't do it I am terrified that I can't what does that say about me. Oxford becomes the kitchen. I resent her for it. How much I love her miss her. Do I mean that? I feel guilt. I fold it into what I know.

We move into **Eimear***'s Art Crit. She is presenting the painting.*

Eimear   I um tried, to make something different but I couldn't. It's just her in the house again. Sorry.

I'll do something better for the final Crit.

. . .

I don't understand the question.

Can you say it again?

Who. Was? She. Before me?

Paint her . . . as a girl? You Mean Outside the house?

But I – That's Not My Thing – What I Paint.

. . .

'*Who was she before you?*'

. . . I don't ? . . .

,

,

Fifty-nine per cent? You can't be serious. Fifty-nine per cent.

*

Gráinne *is having a hot flush. It's like the walls of the home around her have become closer, somehow.*

The phone rings. She dives for it. With her full body.

Gráinne   Eimear? Tom?

Doctor   Hello, is that Mrs Carter? Gray-nee Carter?

Gráinne   Hi, yes it is. It's uh. Gronyuh. Cart–. THANK YOU for your call back.

Doctor   Hi Grayy-nee it's Dr Markley calling here Reigate Medical Pra/ctice

Gráinne   Yep yes hello hello

Doctor   How can I help you today.

Gráinne   Is there a female consultant I could speak to? It's about well it's about my uh.

She whispers.

My um.

Like it's a bad word.

'Body.'

Doctor   Oh, well we want you to feel comfortable. If you /

Gráinne   No it was hard enough to get the appointment no it's fine fine being silly fine

Doctor   Silly ha.

Gráinne   yes never / Hello?

Doctor   Ha. / Sorry the signal's

Gráinne   So I /

Doctor   Well if you're /   **Gráinne**   Sorry you /

Doctor   If you're   **Gráinne**   Sorry

Doctor   Comfortable. Sorry signal

Gráinne   Well. I have. I've um. Yep.

I think there's something very wrong with me and I don't quite know what

Doctor   Oh, right. Well if you'd like to describe for me your symptoms we can go from there

Gráinne   Yes well I feel hot and hotter and hotter and a sort of a strange rage and also quite empty. And then well. I feel strange saying it, Doctor, but it's like my extremities. Little bits of me . . . disappear.

Doctor   So you think you have a temperature

Gráinne   Little bits of me vanish and it's like no one could see me if they looked

Doctor   Are you *saying* you're *seeing* bits of yourself disappear

Gráinne   Yes. I'm saying I'm seeing that. Or not seeing them. Sometimes. My limbs

I don't suppose that's normal is it

,

,

Hello?

Gráinne   Oh you're back   **Doctor**   Your accent is Irish.

Doctor   Lovely. I h/ave   **Gráinne**   Hello?

A friend who's been

To Ireland twice.

Gráinne   I'm physically in a lot of pain

Doctor   Have you been sleeping alright

Gráinne   I get these hot sweats and then I get scared I am going to vanish

Doctor   It sounds like what you are describing is exhaustion

Gráinne   I have been tired before I don't think these are normal sym –

Doctor   Hello? Hello? Sorry, signal

Gráinne *hangs up on the* **Doctor**.

*

Gráinne *dyes her hair.*

Cuts her hair over the sink.

She keeps checking that all of herself is still there.

*

Eimear *phones* **Gráinne**.

Gráinne   Hey, pet! Eimear. Hello!

Eimear   Listen, I can't talk long –

Gráinne   Right

Eimear   But I wanted to come home this weekend and wondered if that's okay.

Gráinne   Oh my GOD yes I will make your bed up nice yes of course. Come for the week. I'll get steak in. The year! I'll go to the nice butchers. Come forever. Yes please. Oh Eimear I can't wait.

WE CAN HAVE THE BEST FOOD

Eimear   I can study

Gráinne   Talk all about university

Eimear   AND WORK ON MY PAINTINGS

Gráinne   It'll be just what I ne/ed

Eimear   Just what I need!

Gráinne *leaps in the air and dances.*

Then does a little prayer.

She puts the radio on and starts to dance. Furiously. Ferociously.

Her arm is still there. Full flesh in the light.

*

Gráinne *is at the Reigate butcher's shop. It's the first time we have seen her leave the house. She has gained confidence from the hope of seeing* **Eimear**. *She's upbeat.*

As **Gráinne** *rifles through her bag to find her wallet, she brings out little gifts.*

Gráinne   Tom always buys me something small and hideous whenever he is gone for long periods. Guilt!

Got this maraca keyring from a stint in Seville. Got this doll from a particularly long time spent in Moscow.

I picture a mistress from every location.

She puts on a fake-English-posh-voice.

Can I have your finest steak, please?

It's for my daughter. She's home from Oxford. Big ones please.

She panics slightly as she pays about whether there's enough on her card.

Nina is Russian. She is older than him by decades and tells him he is a nice little man. This turns him on. She wears garters and has a baby bird she keeps trapped in a cage for sport.

Eleonore is from Paris and I can't quite see her fully. He's not there that often.

From Ireland, well, that was me.

Card please. Contactless? That's great. Thanks.

I imagine one woman in particular whenever he is in Stockholm. She doesn't have a name.

She's bone thin and has long dark hair

She smokes and it doesn't look tragic

She wears a man's blazer

When they fuck she moans like a porn star

Not in a way that's forced

Like she genuinely, actually enjoys it

I imagine their secret dates

The door dings as she leaves the butcher's.

Whisky spilled in grand hotel rooms

He tells her inflated stories of Belfast and The War he didn't fight in

Just there to 'keep the peace', after it's already over –

She doesn't understand and kisses him slowly

Her body hasn't crumbled yet.

I imagine kissing her.

I imagine crushing her skull in my hand.

She unlocks the door back home and starts to clean. The walls are warped; they come in and out of her touch. Or is it her arms?

Act Two

Return

The walls stretch out thin to hold them both, as **Eimear** *returns, but it's like it's impossible for them to be contained in the same space. Things have moved. Changed.*

Gráinne *has done her very best to make the house look perfect for* **Eimear**. *It is spotless.*

The walls are still. **Gráinne** *runs her hand over the surface of the island, just to check, while* **Eimear** *flings her bags and art supplies down.* **Gráinne**'s *arm is still there.*

Eimear's *excitement is huge;* **Gráinne** *tries to reason with her softly, catching at threads.*

Words collide and tumble into each other.

Gráinne   Diesel? Oh I love you / . . .

Eimear   Yeah at first obviously they thought it was better for the environment / !

Gráinne   Does the house look nice?

Eimear   But then obviously there's like that it can cause acid rain /

Gráinne   Do you notice anything different

Eimear   Chairs? Which is obviously Really Bad.

Like Very Bad And Also Antifeminist!

Gráinne   Table's in a different place

Eimear   Yeah it's cute!

Gráinne   Said you liked it better there so I chan/ged it

Eimear   *Quaint*!

Gráinne   Do I look any skinnier?

Eimear   Thanks for picking me up because I can't therefore in good conscience drive ever again!

Gráinne   You don't have a licence.

Eimear   That has nothing to do with it

Surprise!

Eimear *pulls from her bag an enormous bunch of flowers.*

Gráinne   WOW! What are they? WOW

Eimear   Flowers

Gráinne   Yes I know that

(*Slightly panicked.*)

Were they expensive

Eimear   Beautiful, aren't they. Hydrangeas

Gráinne   Yes yes. Get scissors from the drawer please pet.

The two women prepare the flowers. It's strangely awkward. Suddenly and all at once:

Eimear   Tilda loves hydrangeas, she gets them for her Mum every time she goes home. I'd say she's my main Best Friend. She called me that on the phone. I really love it there, Mum, it's like my life is *finally* worth living. I finally have things in life to finally look forward to: Nicaragua, College Formal. And the work's going really well, really good. Have a load of trouble balancing that and my social life because I'm just so busy with the pub and friends all the time. Never have a night off. Ever.

Nope, never.

Gráinne   (Yes, I'm really good thank you for ask) /

Eimear   Sorry?

Gráinne   That's really good, pet, thank you for tell /

Eimear   Oh, no worries.

Gráinne   Makes it all the more special that you're home because you miss your Mummy

Eimear   ,

Need the space have lots of work to do.

Eimear   Love the trousers. And the fruit bowl. Is the Paris painting in a different place

Gráinne   First time I've worn them. Would you like them? If you want them you can have them.

Eimear   I got a first for my first piece

Gráinne *screams. It is inappropriate.*

Eimear *flinches at the scale of the reaction but she soaks the validation.*

Gráinne   OH MY GOD

I AM SO HAPPY YOU'RE HOME

Steak to celebrate. YOU INCREDIBLE GIRL!

Eimear   Oh, I'm not eating

Gráinne   Oh, you'll get hungry later

Eimear   I'm vegetarian now

Gráinne   What?

Eimear   For the environment. And feminism.

Gráinne   Since when

Eimear   Last week

Gráinne   Can you not be vegetarian next week instea –

Eimear   You can't start and stop that's not how it works –

Gráinne   Got them 'cause they're your favourite – our tradition –

Beat, the walls warp. **Eimear** *doesn't notice.*

Gráinne   Not to worry, I can go out and get something in –

The walls come back to fix.

Eimear   Hair's lovely. Darker.

Gráinne   Did it myself!

Eimear   Why

Gráinne (*reflexively*)   Money

She recovers quickly.

Eliot's upped his prices.

Eimear   You missed a bit at the back

Gráinne   Yours is lovely.

Gráinne *goes to touch it.* **Eimear** *smiles apologetically; she doesn't want to upset her.*

Eimear   It'll frizz

Gráinne   It's November

There's a hint of a wall shifting.

Eimear *goes round the back to look at* **Gráinne***'s hair. She starts to paint the root.*

Eimear   Was just saying. We're all going to Nicaragua. For Christmas. Me, Tilda, Fergus and Honor. Tilda is the only person I know who gets the ick for her friends. But not us. It's for an art project around Invisible Labour.

Gráinne   For Christmas? No, no

Eimear   It's charity work – it's philanthropy – it's for the environment.

Gráinne   Kind of her to invite you

Eimear   Yes

Gráinne   I hope she's not disappointed. God it's HOT in here

Eimear   WHAT? I can't go? WHY

Gráinne   Because –

Eimear   But – it's for the environment. It's supporting women out there whose care for their environment otherwise will go undocument –. They're digging holes; they're sacrificing; it's ecofeminism in action.

Gráinne   No

Eimear   Caring for the Earth

If these women don't have their work documented

Have you heard of microbiology

Gráinne   No /

Eimear   It's like where /

Gráinne   No as in No, Eimear, You Are Not Going

Eimear   Already booked my flight

Gráinne   How?

Eimear   Dad's money he sends. I haven't used a lot

Gráinne   YOU'VE. *DAD* IS SENDING Y –

Eimear   Yeah I haven't used a lot I promise. Just a thousand. Flights were free because Tilda's family have a plane but money for my time there and then my formal dress.

Gráinne   He is *sending YOU. Money.*

Eimear *feels bad but chooses to be defensive.*

Eimear   I'm not three. I know you want me to be. Want me where you can see me where you can control me want to stifle me you can't put everything on me. I don't want to be the only girl in my friendship group who can't afford to go.

Gráinne   What about the dress I gave yo/u

Eimear   Matching eyeshadow to go with it. Things you said you wanted for me / –

Gráinne   The dress I gave you to wear

Eimear   Oh I

Gráinne   I gave you the dress I wore when I was – for my *debs* Eimear that my Mam got made from her old dress for me I thought you liked it –

Eimear   I know I know and I love it.

I just

,

Can't find it.

Plus it's not really

the kind of thing my friends are wearing. I'm so sorry

Gráinne   You lost it?

Eimear   I'm sorry I wouldn't mean to ever hur –

I just feel

Doesn't matter

I feel like

You're not making an effort to know the new me.

Can we just leave it. I'm sorry

Can we just leave it.

You don't KNOW me.

Gráinne   ,

I soak your blood-stained underwear in bleach. I put you before everyone, I put you before me. I tell myself you love me. I tell myself you are grateful for everything I do deep down. Somewhere. It's not her fault. I spoil her. If I'd grown up in this. In this house. If I'd been to the schools she went to. Gum-guards and knee-socks. Plato and Pushkin. 'It's Supper, not Dinner, Mummy.' Please use the nicer plates when my friends come round next time. I'd maybe understand where it comes from . . .

You go on and on about these women in fuck knows where but what about your MOTHER. What ABOUT YOUR MOTHER. Does your eco-fuh-eco –

She can't say it; she's too angry.

ECOFUCKINGFEMINISM have room for me?!

Eimear   I don't know what your problem is: Honor's Mum said yes. Can we just leave it you sound so *crazy* when you're angry –

Gráinne   When I was nine I had my head flushed down a toilet. That is my problem. I was kicked in the school playground with adults watching. I shared a room with my sister and we had an orange crate between us. You think you're smart; you think you're talented and you are – you are all of those things my Eimear. But you are not smarter just because you –; I had no chance to go to Art School; I had to earn money right off; I had to drink hot water to stay warm; and I cleaned my Mum's house /

Eimear   OK, I hear you /

Gráinne   every Saturday because she didn't have the energy – I scrubbed butchers' trays from the age of fourteen so that I could buy my family Christmas presents and I love Christmas for that and You Know That and Maybe It *Is* a pride thing but you're telling me you want to disappear to some random country for some random girl and random women and not give your MOTHER a second thought – I would lie down in the street under car-wheels if it unlocked the world for you I gave you nice schools a nice fucking house so you would have the WORLD but you have to let me still be your Mother. Eimear.

I can't care for you when you're like this –

I can't care – can't love you when you're like –

You need to be – you need to be better

Gráinne *bursts out of the house.*

Gráinne   What kind of Mother am I to rage at my child

Eimear   What kind of person am I that no one accepts me

Not Oxford; not school; not even her

Stretch one way to fit one life and I don't quite fill the gap
and I'm too big to squeeze back from where I came from

*

We move with **Gráinne** *to a posh supermarket.*

Gráinne *cups a small amount of cash in her hand. Feverish: it
feels like a waking night-mare.*

Gráinne   Something posh. Quin-o-a. Lentils. What do
vegetarian people *eat*

*She moves around the store. Makes direct eye contact with a
woman,* **Fenella,** *played by* **Eimear.** *She tries to dodge her, still
riling from her argument with* **Eimear,** *until* **Fenella** *intercepts.*

Fenella   Hi Hi.

Gráinne *still tries to skirt around her through the aisle.*

Gráinne   Hello

Fenella   Fenella. Book Club! *Oops You Caught Me*

Gráinne   Faces blending into one today. Sorry, hi

Gráinne *smiles politely, but, still upset tries to move past. To no
avail.*

Fenella   *Oops you've really gone and caught me*

Gráinne *gives up negotiating her way past.*

Gráinne   What are you holding in your hand Fenella

Fenella   *Ooops you caught meee.*

Rose petals.

She winks at **Gráinne.**

For the – you know what.

Gráinne   ?

Fenella   The – you know – lady. Of our age. Stuff.

Darling, you've –

You've got a bit –

She gestures to underneath **Gráinne***'s armpits. They're drenched.*

Gráinne   I had Eimear quite youn–. I'm younger than–Yep.

Fantastic, Fenella. I just really need to. Before the shop
closes –

Fenella *swings her basket around the aisle, looking for a product
for* **Gráinne***, not quite letting her past.*

Fenella   Rose petals. Great for the *hormonesies.*

She winks at **Gráinne** *again.*

Fenella   Goodness. Is it just me or is it hot in here. Ha!
Caught me again.

Have you just begunsies?

Gráinne *is trying to push through;* **Fenella** *is oblivious.*

Gráinne   I just need to get some. Before it clos – Some food
for Eimea –sorry – Fenella?

Fen –

Fenella   Just finding you something for the (pits) – It
happens all the time sweetie don't –

Gráinne   I have to. Before it closes.

Fenella *is blocking the aisle, taking in the rose scent from the bottle.* **Gráinne** *tries to get through again, and snaps.*

Gráinne   FENELLA

Beat as **Gráinne** *realises that she has lost her temper.*

Sorry – I –

Fenella   Darling you're not feeling well are you. I promise you. You feel hostage to your hormones and you can't control how you are and it's like everything shifts around you. But then one day when it all stills it's like total mental clarity. It's hell and then it's heaven.

You wake up one day and you just stop giving a fluff!

Oh fuck it, a fuck!

It's fantastic. I'm transformed!

Sweetie you forgot to pay!

,

*

Eimear *gets her materials and recording device out.*

Eimear   For my End of Term I will paint a landscape. Or a mother who wants to know me and a me who doesn't annoy everyone a-fucking-round me. She is Mum but if she was slightly more steady; and the me is Who I'd Like To Be. Long coat, flat-white on the way to the gallery, knowledgeable without being Too Much. Confident and brave. And this mother does not anger. Our hair is perfectly kept and our skin is made of glass. She listens closely and wants to know *everything*.

Not like Mum and I – We have skin made of orange peel.

Look down at my hands as they work; dish-free; ringed; girl's skin.

Watch them work

I look back up at my canvas and it's shifted. There is only one woman's face and it is changed – younger, not what I just made. I see feathers?

Feathers? Partly covering a young woman's soft face –

I didn't paint this –

Formed from nowhere; as if they've floated along from my pillow along the wall and onto my piece? A young woman's face that isn't mine, isn't the woman I painted either? Isn't Mum's but looks like both of us? She's tied to something, her face as I look up and back is covered in more and more feathers. Her bare chest. In some kind of substance. Some kind of thick, dark sticky substance like liquid coal . . . I see *shame*. I see *a woman's body slumped* on a post I see Belfast I see I see –

*

Gráinne *is working on her computer.* **Eimear** *enters. It is awkward.*

Eimear   Morning Mum –

No response.

Morning.

Gráinne   Just working here, Eimear.

Eimear *doesn't know what to do with herself.*

Eimear   . . .

Eimear *gets a small section of her own work out and picks at it.*

They each sit at opposite ends of the table, their heads buried in their work, eyes trained on what is in front of them. **Eimear** *gets up, unsure what to do.*

After a good, uncomfortable while.

Gráinne   There is Vegan-Shite for breakfast in the cupboard.

Eimear   Thank you.

Eimear *starts to prepare her food, but she hasn't seen some of the items before, and is confused.*

She makes herself a cup of tea instead, watching her mum. Then decides to make **Gráinne** *one too.*

Eimear   I just wanted to say . . .

Gráinne

Eimear   Maybe we both . . .

Gráinne   I don't want to . . .

Gráinne *holds her hand up gently as though to say, 'no'.*

Eimear *places the cup down beside* **Gráinne**.

Eimear   OK . . .

Eimear *is self-conscious, working in front of her.*

She goes up again and tries to make her breakfast. She's struggling.

Gráinne   Wait until it the pan is hot

Eimear   Thanks

Eimear *watches the pan heat up.*

I wanted to say –

Gráinne   I'm working here, pet.

Eimear   How do we (repair) –

Gráinne   I'm working.

(My heart's in bits, Eimear).

Eimear   I'm sorry if I upset you

Gráinne   How do we not /

Eimear   I love you

A long pause.

Eimear   I love you

Gráinne   I love you I will be fine but right now I don't want to (talk) –

A long pause.

Eimear   But if we talk about it we can –

Is it like. A no to the tr(ip) – Sorry. Shouldn't have brought it up –

Gráinne *tries not to spike.* **Eimear** *tries not to anger her.*

Gráinne   Yes, it's a no.

Deflated, but trying to hide it, **Eimear** *sits down.*

They sit in silence again for a while.

Gráinne *stands up and prepares* **Eimear***'s breakfast for her with the vegetarian food.*

She serves it up. Goes back to her laptop. After a few moments, watching **Eimear** *eating alone, puts it back down. Joins her.*

Eimear *(of the food)*   Lovely.

Eimear *slides her plate to* **Gráinne**. **Gráinne** *takes a bite. She doesn't like it but smiles.*

They eat in silence for a little while.

Eimear *stands up and gets the Scrabble set. Without a word, she lays it out for them both to play.* **Eimear** *gestures for* **Gráinne** *to begin playing. She looks at her tiles.* **Eimear** *goes first.*

Eimear   Herald.

Gráinne   Helper.

Eimear   Vary.

Gráinne   Rely.

Eimear   Double letter well done.

,

Sor-ri.

Gráinne   What does that say?

Eimear   Sorry with an I.

Gráinne   ?

Eimear   Sorry with an I. Didn't have a (y)

Gráinne *smiles and laughs. They soften.*

Eimear   I'm struggling with my end of term portrait

Gráinne   That's unlike you.

I'd ask to see it but I know the answer

Eimear   Mum –

Gráinne   Qi. It is one I checked last time –

Eimear   I'm not sure my work is – I don't know if I'm goo –

Have you ever felt like this

Gráinne   Like what

Eimear   Like This

(Like you're seeing bodies blown to bits and feathers)

?

(I didn't think so)

Gráinne   ?

Eimear *stands up.*

Gráinne   I love you

Eimear   I love you

Things still don't feel right.

I need a reference. For the picture. The new one I have a
deadline fo –

Gráinne   Eimear, I –

Eimear   I think I might take the Paris picture back to uni. I need new references for landscapes but it's still on the –

Gráinne   No, no.

You can't just take everything you want from the house.

,

,

NO.

Eimear *goes towards it.*

Gráinne   Eimear, not that (I will have nothing left).

,

,

Eimear   ,

,

Your hair looks lovely Mum.

Gráinne   Thank you

Eimear   Love you

Gráinne   I love you

Eimear   I need a reference. Are you sure I can't? I think it would help me.

They both stare at the painting. **Gráinne** *tries to calmly say no without enraging.*

Eimear *sits back down. They try and finish their Scrabble game.*

Gráinne   I'm stuck.

Eimear *offers her hands to help* **Gráinne** *with her word choice, but her phone rings.*

Eimear   Tilda! Hey. Yeah. No I don't think I can come to a protest tomorrow I told you I'm in Surrey sadly. No just told

her about (Nicaragua). I don't know. Um Yeah – so exciting!
Henry's going is he? Tomorrow? Oh I don't think I can – Tell
him Emma says hi. *Siiiiick*. Love you. Love you more than
anything. Bye!

Gráinne   Eimear

Eimear   Yes

Gráinne   *Emma?*

,

,

,

Eimear *leans across and helps* **Gráinne** *with her word choice.*

Eimear   I said Eimear.

Can I just borrow it for a couple of days? It's where the whole
process of my work start– I need to to go back t–

(I said Eimear)

Tries to distract; fails.

Troubles. The S from Sorr-ih and the R from Rely –

Gráinne   What are you putting that word down for like a
point

You weren't there. You don't know anything about it. We all
moved on why do you bring it up. It's not your business.
You're so worried about it Eimear is the one piece of the
country you have. Don't change your name for some posh
twats –

Eimear   I don't know why I did it

I don't know why I feel so ashamed of everything all the –

I Wish You Would Tell Me Why You're Like This

Why I'm Like This

Mum?

Gráinne *stays still, fading, flickering.* **Eimear** *moves towards* **Gráinne** *but the walls don't let her touch her.*

Eimear, *startled by what is happening, moves towards the painting of Paris. She tries to distract herself. She touches it.*

The walls split open.

*

The walls cough **Eimear** *and* **Gráinne** *into a memory of Ardoyne.*

Gráinne *is watching something meaningless on TV.*

Eimear *watches.*

Gráinne   Mam.

I say three times and on the third time she looks up.

Her eyes are square and her skin is tinted blue by the TV.

Mam.

I say three times and on the fourth time she looks down.

Her hands are old and weary and have not been held in a long time.

What would you do if I got pregnant

When do you think it is acceptable to have sex

She doesn't look up, or down, her eyes just freeze. Then close.

On your wedding night, she spits. Anything earlier you're a whore and any later you're torturing your husband.

Tidy up your paints there, pet. Always making a mess.

Right.

I can feel the shame and shape of Eimear forming in my womb.

I am swaddled in Nana's blanket all in white.

I've been sick three times today but I know the Doctor will tell my Mam.

Mam. I say just once and she looks me in the eye.

'If you've got pregnant, by God, you'd better leave if you know what's good for you' . . .

She takes with her a map, an orange, her deb's dress and her painting of Paris.

I meet Tom at night. I've taken some cash from the till and he's told one friend – not told them my name – that he is *'leaving for honour not 'cause he's a coward'.*

Eimear *enters to try and get to* **Gráinne**, *but the walls throw her back.*

Gráinne   Tom, do you love me?

'You'll love my Mum. Everyone loves Kathy.

She bakes a brilliant strawberry tart and will give you her creamy custard if you're lucky. Kathy's fantastic. Everyone loves Kathy'

I left a note under Ma's pillow which said by God I know what's good for me.

I weep for my Mother but I also weep for Ireland.

I weep for the Irish children I will not raise.

I weep all the way across the channel whilst Tom looks out to sea.

I thought if I could change the wallpaper in Tom's Mum's nursery that would make it feel more like home

I thought if I opened the windows and changed the environment I would find out what it is I am meant to be doing

I imagine the great golden well of love I have for her, kicking in my womb

I vow now to never raise my voice or swear at her

Eimear *moves to leave the house, panicked, but is guided, moved or pushed by the walls back to her paints. Closed in further to the home by the walls.*

*

She tries to paint what she just saw, but looks down and the canvas has moved again. She tries to steady herself, but the walls burst completely open.

She steps through, alarmed. She tries to push against the walls but it's no use.

Gráinne *plays* **Mam**. *She is on the phone to her own mother, trying to tell her about the tarring and feathering.*

Gráinne   Ma? It's Clíodhna here. Sorry for the late-night call.

Listen, I'm worried sick about wee Gráinne.

She's not been eating properly since she. Saw.

Since she *saw,* Mammy.

I thought you would have heard, or seen it in the –

Oh,

I thought Da would have told you.

I was – It was . . . I know it's best not to speak on difficult things.

It is important too that you – know.

After the hijacking, sure I told you about that.

How UVs took hold of the wheel of our car down by Crumlin Road

And drove it, round by Flax Street

Put their hands over our mouths, then bags over our heads, even without sight we felt their guns pointed towards us –

Until they used them to open fire on –

I am sorry, Ma, I know it is difficult to hear about that –

There's a sense in Belfast that rage is renewing itself

And leaking out into the home.

It's infecting relationships with the women and children. How they see us

I know it's best not to speak about these things but the women are feeling the hard stick of it more and more.

INLA men. They heard that I was in the car when their boys were shot at

And decided that made me . . . That that made me

Baseless as it was. That it made me a loyalist spy

It has no logic, Mammy, but a group of them stormed our house

Took me into the street and . . .

She finds it very difficult to say it.

Well they attached my skirts to the lamppost, hung by from the waist

They ripped my top and

Covered me in tar.

She can barely speak.

And smothered feathers.

The whole street watched from their windows

Wee Gráinne saw it all

And it was my fault for speaking about the hijacking I must have told someone I was in the car then word spreads shifts changes into lies I will not talk about it again.

Yes of course I'll *'get on with it'*.

Of *course* I'll

I won't mention it to her again.

Make like it never happened. You're right Ma

You're right, of course.

Ma. She's listening on the stairs. I have to go.

Eimear, *now fully conscious of and terrified by the shifting walls, makes to run. To leave. They won't let her.*

They keep guiding her back to her painting.

She pauses. Considers. Something from deep within her takes over.

Her art becomes urgent; embodied; her panic distils into focus.

She paints and folds and paints.

Until it emerges.

A young girl.

Gráinne. *In full detail. Sat outside the steps of her school in Ardoyne.*

She holds the painting up.

We see her in full colour.

The walls let her go.

The walls still and form a more stable, but still split, formation.

She realises she is free.

But creates one last painting of **Gráinne**, *that we don't see. Covers her work in cloth.*

Eimear *grabs her closest things: her phone, her bag and turns back quickly for an orange.*

The walls look like they might move again.

Startled, **Eimear** *leaves.*

Act Three

Gone

Gráinne *is peeling an orange in the doctor's waiting room.*

Gráinne Something about calling the Doctor makes me want to shrink out of my skin but I cannot be the mother who rages at her daughter. Talking about my body makes me feel violent or violently ill. Makes me want to lash out or fall through the floor. But I am doing it for her.

Fenella *sits down and beams at* **Gráinne**. *For a few moments,* **Gráinne** *avoids eye contact, and we think she'll get away with it, until* **Fenella** *forces herself into view.*

Fenella Hi Hi

Gráinne Fucking Fenella

Fenella *Oops you caught me*

Gráinne Just brilliant to see you this early

Fenella We've missed you in Book Club. Wondered if you'd been feeling

She whispers.

Poorly

Gráinne I've been working

Not meaning to be patronising, but failing.

Fenella So inspiring that you work.

Are you here for a check-up. Do you Care To Share.

Sharing. Is. Caring. As they say in the Czech Republic.

Gráinne Just, stuff

Fenella The Menny-P.

Gráinne   I'm sorry?

Fenella *winks at* **Gráinne**. **Gráinne** *doesn't stir.* **Fenella** *realises she is going to have to be more specific.*

Fenella   The meno ------------

pause.

She dramatically stops, as if a gong has been sounded that **Gráinne** *can't hear.*

Fenella   Time for reflection.

Our last book in book club was by Davina McCall.

You missed it.

Gráinne   Gutted

Fenella   You're Peri, aren't you. Another woman can always tell. I have a good eye for it. Good nose.

Here's my cheat-sheet. I made it for all the ladies after book club. We all felt like we were going through it alone but we weren't. Felt insane but we're not. It's changing Gráinne but we still have a fight on our hands. It was Candida-Grace who told me all of this before she fucked off back to uni. Here, sweetie, take it.

Gráinne   No that's –

Fenella   Guess how many women in the world are prescribed it.

Gráinne   ?

Fenella   Go on guess. It's my Favourite Fact I learned it myself

Gráinne   I don't know

Fenella   Oh go on, guess

Gráinne *opens her mouth to speak.*

Fenella   Five! Five per-fluffing-per cent.

You'll have to fight for it. Read it before you go in. Some of them aren't trained to know what to look for. My phone number's on the back. You can call me anytime sweetie and I will always pick up.

Gráinne *leaves the appointment before it starts, freaked out.*

*

Gráinne *returns home and can't see* **Eimear** *anywhere.*

She sees the painting of Paris which has come off the wall and, shaken, reinstates it.

Gráinne   Eimear? Eimear?

No response from anywhere she looks.

Emma?

No response.

EIMEAR.

No response.

She feels for her face. It isn't there.

She tries to find it in spoons and mirrors and surfaces but it's gone.

She can't find her phone again. After pulling everything she has cleaned apart, and muddying everything somehow in her search, she finds her phone. Calls **Eimear***.*

Eimear   MUM. Hello?

Gráinne   Eimear, where are you pet?

Eimear   I'm so sorry, I'm feeling really weird I felt very strange things were –

I'm on my way back to Oxford

Gráinne   For the protest

Eimear   Well, sort of but mainly –

Gráinne   You're on the train?

Eimear   No, Uber. I was feeling so weird Mum it was like –

Gráinne   How much was that then, Eimear –

Eimear   The – Mum the *hou–*. I want to expla –

Gráinne *is speechless. She puts the phone down and doesn't even hang up.*

Eimear's *speech is muffled.*

After a while – and after a hot flush – she picks the phone back up.

Gráinne   Come home

Gráinne *is speechless. She puts the phone back down.*

Eimear's *speech is muffled.*

After a while – and after a hot flush – she picks the phone back up.

Eimear *is gone.*

She puts the phone down and feels her face but it's still there – for now. Glitchy.

She deliberately pours **Eimear**'s *stale coffee cup onto the floor and messes up her hangers. Eyes up her cleaning products. She turns pillows over and knocks over her perfume and makeup.*

She is having a hot flush.

Gráinne   I order Swedish food and I gorge on it

I buy a long dark wig from Amazon made of dog hair

She's shoving Swedish food into her mouth.

I decide that Tom will come home from Stockholm

That I will make him

She's shovelling it in now.

I wonder what her name is, this Swedish lover whose existence I have created but makes my chest pound, wrinkles feel thick with the burden of her elasticity . . .

I find a Swedish name generator and take the first option

I look at every Anna Lagerqvist who posts on Facebook

And fill their inboxes with hate

Shoving food now.

Zoom in on every pore

Find a flaw in all of their smiles

Or perhaps he's brought Eleonore with him. The French woman whose face I cannot picture . . .

She has a stomach cramp and stares at herself in the mirror.

She leaves the house. It's like the light is too bright for her eyes.

She walks and walks past shops until she gets to the doctor's surgery. She tries to go in but can't – the doors aren't automatic. She pounds at them until she is let in.

She walks to the front of the queue.

Gráinne   Yes. That's. Gráinne. G-R-A-I-N-N-E. Like Granny if you were dyslexic. (That's) What my husband (says).

1979. 06. 06. 82.

She is seated in the doctor's chair now.

Yes.

Yes.

I have one child.

She's eighteen. She's um. At Oxford. Ruskin. In Oxford.
Now.

Well it feels sort like a general scraping like a knife or like
barbed wire /

And my skin is hot very hot

And I have been bleeding for nineteen days

,

,

I'd say that *is* an emergency

My quality of life is stuck in this cycle of when the pain
comes and goes; I am unable to think straight it's like a fog –
like there's this hot mist in my head and I am irritable, and I
can't I don't know what's real

It *feels* pretty serious, doctor.

And I'm only forty-three and I don't know if it's just the
menopause or stress but I can't think straight I can't

I need something to

Take away the –

I need HRT, basically

,

,

,

What do you mean no

Do you have a mother, Doctor?

Feel like your insides started crumbling at thirty-nine

Feel like you can't even recognise your own reflection

Like you have entirely disappeared

Can you even see me anymore

Can you hear me

What do you mean national shortage

How can you be short of something 51 per cent of women will need

Just produce more

Produce fucking more

Where is the chemist where is it make them give it to me I can't even can't even think –

She flips a table.

She does anything to make herself seen.

She tries to hypnotise him by talking slowly.

GIVE. ME. HRT.

Please.

The doctor won't.

She leaves the office and pounds on the door of the butcher's.

They are not open.

She goes into a shop and finds a dress that she thinks might suit **Eimear**. *She tries it on.*

Gráinne   It's for my daughter's formal but we are the same size – well she's a bit smaller but roughly the same –

She's at Oxford. So. Yeah.

Gráinne *goes to the till to pay. She taps her debit card.*

Declined.

Shocked, she tries again. And again.

She rifles through her bag; through Tom's gifts, to find a cash wallet.

She counts, panicked, and has just enough. Hands it over.

She rises hot.

You don't – sorry. Know anywhere I could um. Buy HRT . . . Illegally. I don't know if that's something you young folk would deal but if you have a dealer who could . . .

JOKING. I'm joking I'm desperate. Ha.

She looks down at herself and winces.

What she's wearing. What she's doing.

A pause, as she comes to and realises her situation.

A pure flood of emotion comes over her. Properly feeling, with no defence or coping mechanisms distracting her.

She picks up the phone. It rings for a few beats, and then the call goes through.

Gráinne   Fenella?

*

Gráinne *and* **Fenella** *stand over the kitchen island.* **Fenella** *doesn't ask a single question about the dress* **Gráinne** *is wearing.* **Fenella** *has a full array of hormone patches and products.*

Fenella　We've been stockpiling them for a while, a couple of the girls from Book Club. Ever since the National Shortage. A few of the girls are *Doctors*.

Gráinne　Really?

Fenella　I know, so inspiring that they work.

Gráinne *tries very hard to seem relaxed.*

Fenella　They don't solve everything, SweetieFace, but they go some way.

Gráinne *smiles at* **Fenella**.

Fenella　I'm leaving him

Gráinne　– Who

Fenella　I'm leaving Tarq, you know.

Gráinne　No?

Fenella　I'm going to work for a charity. Women's health. In Berlin.

I went to Imperial. Did you know that?

And I always wanted to do it.

But Tarq wanted a wife, Mummy wanted me married and life got in the way.

Nice painting.

Eimear's?

Half embarrassed; half shocked someone noticed.

Gráinne　Mine, actually

Fenella   See where she gets it from

Gráinne   Oh, I'm *no* good compared to –

Fenella   You are. Candie-Grace said Eimear always talks about it. How she gets it from you.

Paris. Haven't been for ages

Gráinne   I've never been.

Fenella *helps* **Gráinne** *with the HRT patch.* **Fenella** *slips away. The walls move as her hormones shift, and take* **Gráinne** *to Ardoyne.*

*

Gráinne   Lazarus. Look mam. That's –

Mam   Not a valid word.

Pause.

Niall O'Hara's had a break in. Not a lot to steal Lord bless his sweet soul but the trauma of it, you know.

Did you ever think about dating is son, wee Cian O'Hara? He's a little short but has a sweet smile and –

Are you seeing anyone, pet

Gráinne   No. Never am.

Pause

Mam   It's just you haven't been home much.

It's just ever since you started spending more time down the butcher's it's felt like

I never see you, pet.

It's felt like I'm. Well. Like I'm losing you, sort of.

She's counting up her Scrabble pieces. Stops.

I just thought maybe you had met someone. You don't want to be down the butcher's forever.

And you could bring him into the fold and then you'd spend more time with me

If we could all spend time together.

But not to worry

I bet you it was one of those garrison soldiers posted down Bessbrook who broke into Niall O'Hara's nice wee house. Keeping the peace. Keeping the peace after it's all already over. What kind of –

Oh, I bet you it was. The filth.

Gráinne   They're just lost boys a lot of them, Mam

Mam *doesn't look at her, just carries on.*

Mam   I bet you it was one of 'em

I just wish you'd be home more, pet

My life is empty without you

I love you more than anyone will ever love you

More than anything in the world

Gráinne   Mammy, I'm sorry about what hap – I would find it hard too.

Mam   We don't speak of it, pet. We move on. You weren't there. Had nothing to do with you.

Gráinne *goes to leave.*

Mam   If you're heading out, wee pet. Take an orange with you

*

Gráinne *returns back to the present day. She takes off the prom dress and hangs it up in* **Eimear**'s *room. She steps around the stuff she has broken.*

She stumbles across a scrabble piece in one of **Eimear**'s *shoes. Looks at it. A flash of Mammy.*

She goes to her phone. Hands shaking. Types numbers in.

To her total shock, someone picks up.

Gráinne   Mam. It's me. Hi. Oh wow. It's Gráinne. It's your wee girl.

Mam's Husband   Hello?

Gráinne *is confused.*

Mam's Husband   Hello

Gráinne   Who is this? Who's speaking

Mam's Husband   Peter O'Hara

Gráinne   ?

Peter as in Niall's cousin Peter who mowed the lawn sometimes

Mam's Husband   . . . Gráinne?

Gráinne   What are you doing answering the home phone? Is she there can you pass her on

Mam's Husband   She's not here

Gráinne   Will you ever just pass her on please.

Mam's Husband   She's not here, pet

Gráinne   Will you please

Long pause. What he is about to say becomes somehow obvious.

Mam's Husband   She's passed on.

I thought you would have heard.

Gráinne   No I uh – I hadn't

Mam's Husband   Not since

Gráinne   Not since Eimear no

Mam's Husband   Who

Gráinne   How are you – you have our home phone

Mam's Husband   We married.

Gráinne   Oh.

Mam's Husband   The year after you left. She was broken, Gráinne.

The shame.

In her later years looked on it more kindly tried to look you up but she'd nothing to go on you left no trac –

Gráinne   I'm sorry?

Mam's Husband   I should thank you though, for staying away. Never making her think about it much. She was happy. She was happier.

She stays stunned by the phone.

After a little while. After gathering herself.

She calls **Eimear**.

Gráinne   Eimear I am going to tell you about Ireland. About my life before you.

Will you give me a call back. When you want to.

*

Eimear *is at the protest in Oxford.*

Eimear   Home I have found here

Amongst people who think like me

A whole new world we find in our discussions

they're not anxious about keeping me containing me

I am desperate to keep them

But they don't love me fiercely like she does

They have an apathy for me

And yet

I feel so alive as we march; placards in our hands we painted

Swarms of young women coming together; soft power

Tilda takes my hand and whispers Henry wants to see me later

The world is so much bigger than Reigate or worrying or the way the house makes me go crazy like I'm seeing things

I feel electric alive pulsing stretches of possibility new new new give me new

Books to read; food to eat; people to meet to dance with shaking off the way

I felt about my body when Mum asked if she was skinny yet

When Louis Ivor called me frigid

When people in Surrey judged and judged here I'm judged for my potential

Darting through people ow sorry sorry got to get to Henry

Why do I feel guilty

Elbows placards screams of OUR HOUSE IS ON FIRE

Why do I feel guilty

Mum oh Gosh oh no why Do I Feel So Guilty

Swallow three times and it's OK; and there is Henry

My new home. He's in my new

Flat and as he takes off my jumper

And then my top I feel so so alive

Like I am being looked at properly by

The gaze I so want for the first time

And It Is Good We Both Enjoy It I Feel

Like I am coming into the light

I feel guilty

Stepping into view being seen

Wanted; touched

He Says My Name, Emma,

I Say Henry It's Eimear

And it is Great and it is Light it is fleeting I know that but it's fun and it's helping me become myself but

I want the purity of my Mum's love too

I shouldn't have left

I'm so hotheaded

Like Her

*

Gráinne, *changed and looking a little more put together, enters the Reigate butcher's shop.*

Butcher Shop Man   Hi

Gráinne   Hi

Butcher Shop Man   Hi

Gráinne   SORRY it's just you look a little um

Butcher Shop Man   Hmm?

Gráinne   Familiar.

Beat.

I'm just after some meat.

Butcher Shop Man   Yep. . .

Gráinne   Obviously. Sorry.

Steaks. I'm after. Steaks. Big ones. Big ones please.

Are you. You're not. Where are you. Where is it you're from

Butcher Shop Man   France.

Gráinne   Oh. Uh, me too. Kind of. Not really. I have um a French – name.

Butcher Shop Man   Which is?

Beat

Gráinne   Eleonore. Where in France are you from

He's packaging up her steaks. Hands them to her. She pulls out the objects from her bag from earlier and finds Eleonore's beret.

Butcher Shop Man   Paris

Gráinne   What's it like

Butcher Shop Man   Icy and hot. Beautiful.

She stares at him. Feels a flicker of something. Is it attraction? Promise?

Gráinne   And the people

Butcher Shop Man   Keep themselves to themselves

Gráinne   The wine

Butcher Shop Man   Second to none.

She thinks.

Gráinne   Thank you.

And if you wanted to disappear –

Butcher Shop Man   I'm sorry

Gráinne   For a while. At least.

Could you.

He doesn't answer her.

As he turns his back to take a phone call, she grabs a load of money from the till. And the steaks.

She leaves.

*

Gráinne, *glitching, fading in and out, stumbles into the kitchen. Lays out the steaks.*

Pushes the bowls of oranges over and rearranges them on the floor with the scrabble pieces. It is artful. She grabs Tom's gifts and folds them into the painting. Beautiful, whatever way she moves them and whatever it is she makes. She lingers on the beret of Eleonore's, puts it next to her painting of Paris on the wall.

She starts to paint with the blood of the steaks and create something messy and wonderful and free.

Then goes to **Eimear**'s *bedroom.*

She takes off **Eimear**'s *dress and lays it down on her bed. She kisses it.*

She starts to tidy **Eimear**'s *messy bedroom and sees her tape recorder and art materials she has left in her room.*

She flicks through the portfolio, and plays the tapes.

They're tender, many of them, beautiful.

She is moved. Shocked by how much **Eimear** *thinks of her. And in the latest ones, sees her. How much she talks in the tapes of shame.*

Gráinne   Wee pet

I just wanted to let you know I'm going.

I am so sorry. I love you.

I'm going to go and spend some time in Paris.

Kid, you see, for the longest time I have felt like I am disappearing. And medicine's good and all but I need to do something for myself.

I think I have been worried to say it to you out loud but it seems some way or another you know.

When I was four years old, Mammy's car was hijacked by the loyalists and then an unspeakable thing happened to her. It changed the way she saw her body and it changed the way I saw mine.

I think I have carried that on my shoulders and I think I brought her more shame. Thought I was leaving for Mammy's shame but it had become my own

I think . . .

I have buried it in the walls of the work I have done for you and in the foundations of the life we built here but never fought it head on.

When we avoid things they come back up; don't they; find horrible new roots in the people we love

Wee pet, when you come home I will be gone but I don't want you to worry yourself.

I want you to go to wherever crazy place you're headed and have the most wonderful time. I would have done the same thing if I'd the life chances you have.

Wee pet, you see. I have sacrificed and it has been invisible to you

I have given everything but I have also given shame that's clouded your vision so you can't see the good I've done

I have

Allowed my shoulders to hurt with the legacy of where they've hurt for centuries

Carrying the pain of our mothers of our mothers' mothers' mothers. It's not ours is it pet

I am going to have new adventures and I will be back at some point I promise you. I love you. I think I will go by the name of Eleonore and I might even paint again. Made a fucking mess downstairs didn't I but I Feel Like I Am Becoming Me

Because my Eimear

We are from a country of fucking incredible strong people

Brave people who have accepted other people's shame as their own

So

If I am going to disappear, I am going to have some fucking say in where I'm going

If they are not going to not see me it's going to be my fucking choice.

I disappeared the moment my medicine was refused

I disappeared the moment I turned thirty and then forty then

I lived like my life was done to me but

I have chances my Mammy didn't have

Things are different for me and they will be for you

Now it's mine

It's mine

My going

If I'm going it is My

Choice

My going

Bit by bit the limbs from **Eimear***'s artwork come to life and restore her.*

The walls of the home move at her will. She bends the shape of the home into something subtly new. Beautiful.

We watch her leave for Paris, taking the beret from Tom's woman, Eleonore. She places her own painting from the kitchen of Paris on **Eimear***'s bed, with the tape recorder over it.*

We see the daylight fade on the painting on **Eimear***'s bed.*

Time passes.

We see **Eimear** *return. Look for her mum.*

We see her move around the house, look at the pile of steak and oranges that have been strewn into **Gráinne***'s artwork. She picks them up tenderly.*

She goes into her room and sees the beautiful formal dress first, and is incredibly moved.

She sees the painting. She picks up the tape recorder, left in an odd place, with a Post-it note, 'listen, pet'. We see her play **Gráinne***'s tape. Soak it in.*

We see her unsheathe a perfect, life-like painting of her mum, in which she is a fierce warrior. We see her place the tapes in **Gráinne***'s hand in the painting. She is holding them like a sword.*